WILD GOOSE PRINTS

no.2

SKETCHES AND SCRIPTS FOR WORSHIP AND DISCUSSION

JOHN L. BELL & GRAHAM MAULE

These scripts may be used in worship or for discussion purposes. All are based on the life and teaching of Jesus and the experience of his people.

First Published 1986
Second Edition 1988

CONTENTS

The Wild Goose is a Celtic symbol of the Holy Spirit
It serves as the logo of Iona Community Publications

WILD GOOSE PUBLICATIONS
The Publishing Division of The Iona Community

Pearce Institute, 840 Govan Road, GLASGOW G51 3UT
☎ (041) 445 4561

© 1988 The Iona Community   ISBN 0 947988 10 6

INTRODUCTION

The first collection of Gooseprints *Wild Goose Prints No. 1* concentrated mainly on short scenes from the New Testament set in contemporary Scottish vernacular. In the second collection we hope the material will be accessible to a wider readership, all of the pieces being, in the main, in standard English.

There are still, of course, regional variations. 'Aye', will in different vicinities, require to be changed to 'Yes'; while a word like 'folk' may have to be rendered 'people' in those parts of Britain where the former word seems out of place.

It will also be necessary, depending on the denomination of the users, to alter words like 'Communion Table' to 'altar' and 'minister' to 'priest' or 'vicar' as suits. Where such alterations would enable the scripts to take root in local culture, they should be made.

There are two new types of material included in this collection. One is the short play, of which *I Beg Your Pardon* and *Question Time* are the examples. We include them because our own progression was from small two-people dialogues to larger extended pieces and because several colleagues suggested that we should publish them. They require not much more by way of props, but considerably more by way of dramatic experience if they are to be performed rather than merely read.

We have also included a collection of discussion starters – the four *Death Conversations*. These have been used in R. E. and Social Education classes in secondary schools with good effect as catalysts to conversation on a topic which young people are rarely allowed to explore honestly.

We hope that, as with *Wild Goose Prints No. 1*, these scripts will provoke and amuse. But they will fail if that is all that they do. We hope that they will be tools for evangelism, especially to those for whom evangelism has hitherto failed.

John L. Bell
Graham Maule

THE INCARNATION

This script may be used in complete absence of movement, simply by positioning the three voices in different parts of the hall or church and having the dialogue appropriately interspersed with simple lines of music. This would allow for evocative slides to be shown to accompany the words.

More commonly, the script has involved groups of people miming actions in keeping with the words of the two narrators while God sits aloof on a ladder, eventually coming down to creation in the closing sentences.

In either case, the sketch is best followed immediately by a song, preferably beginning before the actors or readers leave the stage. Before The World Began *from* Wild Goose Songs – Volume 1 *is most suitable.*

NARRATOR A : God looked around and saw the world which he had made
a long time ago. And what he saw upset him.

In one place preachers were talking about peace,
    priests were talking about peace,
    prophets were talking about peace.
So much talking,
but there was no peace.
There was only talking to hide the noises of war.

God sighed a heavy sigh. *(God sighs)*

NARRATOR B : In another place people were building,
    building banks and storehouses,
    building monuments to their own greed,
    building meat mountains and butter mountains.
So much building,
while the poor became poorer
and the scales of justice were biased to the rich.

God sighed a heavy sigh. *(God sighs)*

NARRATOR A : In another place people were doing their own thing,
    doing their own thing about loving,
    doing their own thing about trusting,
    doing their own thing about healing.

So much doing their own thing,
But the truth was
That nothing was being done,
For all were divided, suspicious and lonely.

God sighed a heavy sigh. *(God sighs)*

NARRATOR B : In another place, people were worshipping,
        worshipping what their hands had made,
        worshipping what their money had bought,
        worshipping what their fantasies had imagined.
So much worshipping,
but no faith and no hope and no God.

God sighed a heavy sigh. *(God sighs)*

Then he stopped sighing and got angry,
and said,

GOD : I'm fed up.
There's only one answer to this mess –
I'm going to destroy the world!

NARRATOR A : Then God thought for a minute
and he began to cry.
And through the tears he said,

GOD : How can I kill those who were born out of my love?
I am God, not a man.
I will not destroy.
I will save the world.
I will let the world know that I love it.

NARRATOR A : So God got to thinking:

GOD : How can I tell my people that I love them?

NARRATOR A : God's first thought was telepathy.

GOD : I'll just think about it.
I'll sit down and think about it
and if they read my thoughts,
they'll know how I feel.

NARRATOR A : So God sat down, and thought and thought,
but people had other things on their minds.

GOD : So much for telepathy,

NARRATOR A : said God.

NARRATOR B : God's second thought was sign language.

GOD : I'll make some signs to show that I love them,
then they'll understand and things will turn for the better.

NARRATOR B : So God made some signs . . .
like . . . a rainbow.

GOD	:	*(Sings)* "Somewhere over the rainbow . . ."
NARRATOR B	:	But nobody understood. Then he made another sign by opening the Red Sea to let his people escape from slavery.
GOD	:	*(Sings)* "If you go down to the sea today, you're sure of a big surprise . . ."
NARRATOR B	:	And the people were impressed, but nobody really understood. Then he made another sign: he gave them food in the desert.
GOD	:	*(Sings)* "Food glorious food, cold manna for breakfast . . ."
NARRATOR B	:	And everybody ate, but nobody really understood. Nobody understood any of God's signs.
GOD	:	So much for sign language,
NARRATOR B	:	said God.
NARRATOR A	:	God's third thought was telegrams. For these he needed messengers whom he called prophets. And they each received telegrams, some with few words, some with many words. They were to read these to the people.
PROPHETS *(or Narrator B)*	:	Words, words, words, words, words.
NARRATOR A	:	But, for all the words, nobody understood; or, if they did, they didn't let on.
GOD	:	So much for telegrams,
NARRATOR A	:	said God. Then God thought about using the Telephone, but when he discovered the cost of trunk calls, he decided not to bother. God sighed a heavy sigh. *(God sighs)*
NARRATOR B	:	Then God had a brainwave . . .
GOD	:	I'll send . . . I'll send . . . I'll go there myself . . . . . but how?
NARRATOR A	:	God called a meeting of his three selves . . . the Creator, the Word and the Spirit.

6

GOD	:	I move the Word goes,
NARRATOR B	:	said the Creator.
GOD	:	I second that, *(using a different accent)*
NARRATOR B	:	said the Spirit.
GOD	:	Wait a minute ! *(using a different accent)*
NARRATOR B	:	said the Word.
NARRATOR A	:	But there was no minute, for there was no time. So the Word became flesh: tiny and frail flesh, nappy wet and girning flesh, bone of our bone, flesh of our flesh, the son of Joseph and Mary.

* * * * * * *

7

GOD THE FATHER?

Two people stand or sit apart. PAT should be located behind a lectern or table flicking through the back pages of a large pulpit bible. DON may move towards PAT if it is felt appropriate. Either part may be played by a male or female.

DON	:	Are you going to read the Bible?
PAT	:	No . . . I'm just looking. *(He/she flicks through the back pages)*
DON	:	Is it Revelation you're interested in?
PAT	:	No . . . Why?
DON	:	Because it's the last book in the Bible and you seem to be looking at the back pages.
PAT	:	It's the index I'm looking for actually.
DON	:	Why's that?
PAT	:	If you must know, I'm trying to find out how many times God is called Father.
DON	:	Is it a competition you're entering?

(No response)

Are the Brownies trying to raise money to buy a new toadstool?

(No response)

Is it for the organ fund?

PAT	:	Don, what are you going on about?

DON	:	Well, sometimes church organisations have quizzes. If they're not allowed to try people's luck, they test their intelligence. You know the kind of thing:
		      How old was Methusaleh when he died?
		      How many wives had Abraham?
		      How often is God called 'Father' in the Bible?
		Hand in the quiz sheet with 50 pence to the Sunday School Superintendant next Sunday morning . . .

PAT	:	*(Looks and pauses)* No !
DON	:	Well, why are you looking up how many times God is called Father?

PAT	:	Because it's beginning to get to me.
DON	:	It's beginning to get to you ? ? ? ?
PAT	:	Don, for years I've said the Lord's Prayer, like you − 'Our Father which art in Heaven', and it's never bothered me. But we have a new minister and when he prays it's "Father this and Father that!"
DON	:	Is that unusual?
PAT	:	And worst of all, if he's saying grace, he says "With a father's gifts grant us also a father's blessing" . . . a father's blessing ! !
DON	:	But what's wrong with that? Why get het up about a grace?
PAT	:	*(Very directly)* Don . . . if God is like a father . . . is he like your father or my father?
DON	:	I don't understand.
PAT	:	I don't know what the word 'father' means to you, but I know what it means to me.
		My father is the man I never see,
		Because he's either working late, or he's at the Masons,
		or he's out at some committee of the church.
		'Your father's a busy man . . .' that's what people say to me.
		And so he is . . . too busy to talk to his own children,
		and too busy to talk to his own wife,
		but he shouts at her . . .
		When he thinks we're out he shouts at my mother and when I appear and ask what's up, he says "It's alright",
		but I know it's all wrong!

(Pause)

		My father tells lies.
DON	:	I didn't know that, Pat.
PAT	:	So, when I hear our minister going on about God being like a father pitying his children, I think of how my father ignores his children.
		And when he asks for a father's blessing . . . I remember that it's a mother's blessing I want.
DON	:	But God's not like that.
PAT	:	Not like a mother?
DON	:	No. Not like a father . . . I mean . . . not like your father, Oh, in any case Pat, it's only words.
PAT	:	Words to you Don.
		But to me it's my family . . . . . and my faith.

* * * * * *

9

DEATH CONVERSATIONS

These four conversations may be either read or acted. If used in a school or youth group setting, it is best to pause after each one and allow for discussion which arises from points in the experience of the class or group which are relevant to the dialogue.

1. THE PATIENT

(Scene: A Waiting Room in a Hospital)

ALASTAIR : Well, who's going to tell him . . . you or me?

BRIAN : Do you think there's a choice?

ALASTAIR : Well, I might be his brother, but you're his best friend.

BRIAN : What about Margaret, his wife?

ALASTAIR : Listen, Brian, it's a man's job,
Margaret would just break down
and the last thing we want is tears.

BRIAN : And are you sure that you'll be able to control yourself?

ALASTAIR : Who said it was going to be me?

BRIAN : Well, you are his brother.

ALASTAIR : Aye, but you're his best friend.

(Pause)

ALASTAIR : How long did the doctor say he had to go?

BRIAN : I don't know, it was you who spoke to him.

ALASTAIR : Right enough . . . he mentioned three months at the most, six weeks at the least.

BRIAN : So the sooner we tell him the better?

ALASTAIR : I don't know, Brian.
I don't know that our Jack would want to know.

BRIAN : But surely he'll have some idea . . . with the tests and the tubes and being moved to the door of the ward.
He's maybe ill, but he's not daft, Alastair.

ALASTAIR	:	No . . . he's not daft. But I think if it was me, I wouldn't want to know.
BRIAN	:	But it's not you . . . it's him. So what'll we do?
ALASTAIR	:	You say 'we' . . . do you think we should tell him together?
BRIAN	:	Maybe it was a slip of my tongue.

(Pause)

ALASTAIR	:	There's always the doctor. I think he should tell him. I mean, he's the medical expert, he can answer all the questions.
BRIAN	:	Aye, but it's maybe not medical questions Jack will want to ask.
ALASTAIR	:	Do you mean we should get a minister to tell him?
BRIAN	:	It might not be religious questions he wants to ask.
ALASTAIR	:	What kind of questions then are you talking about?
BRIAN	:	I don't know if I'm talking about questions at all. It might be that he'll want to say some things to us about his life, try to clear his mind, try to get us to understand the bits about him that he's always kept to himself.
ALASTAIR	:	Here, that's a bit heavy.
BRIAN	:	So is death.
ALASTAIR	:	Brian, there's no need to be morbid.
BRIAN	:	No, Alastair, and there's no need to be scared of what's natural.
ALASTAIR	:	So, who's going to tell him . . . you or me . . . or Margaret, or the doctor, or us all, or none of us at all?

2. THE BODY

(Scene: A Waiting Room, as above)

MARGARET :	Well, are you going to.
ALASTAIR :	Going to what?
MARGARET :	Going to go in and see him?
ALASTAIR :	But he's not there any more.
MARGARET :	I know, but the doctor said we could go in and see him if we wanted.
ALASTAIR :	I think you'd best do that on your own.
MARGARET :	Will you go later?
ALASTAIR :	I'll think about it.
BRIAN :	I'll go in with you Margaret, I'd like to see him at peace.
ALASTAIR :	So, are you going to leave me out here on my own?
BRIAN :	Come in with us if you like.
ALASTAIR :	No . . . I'm sure it's a private thing.
BRIAN :	I always go to see the body, I think it's very important.
ALASTAIR :	How come?
BRIAN :	Well, it let's you know that he's dead.
MARGARET :	When I was wee, my mother took me in to see the old man next door. I was only about four. He was lying there all in white. She said 'Go and give Mr. Patterson a kiss, Margaret, and you'll not be afraid of dead people ever again'.
ALASTAIR :	Margaret, that's terrible! !
MARGARET :	No, it was quite all right, it wasn't terrible. Have you never seen a corpse, Alastair?
ALASTAIR :	Well I have . . . in the films . . . you know the news reports from Ethiopia or Nicaragua, but never live . . . I mean . . . dead.
MARGARET :	Well, there's always a first time.
ALASTAIR :	Aye, but maybe not this time.
BRIAN :	Are you going to let the kids see their daddy, Margaret?
MARGARET :	Do you think I should Alastair?
ALASTAIR :	It's nothing to do with me . . . you're their mother.
MARGARET :	Aye, and you're their uncle, and if they go and you don't how will you feel? And how will they feel?

12

ALASTAIR : Do you think it's important to see him then, Margaret?
Do you think it's important to see him, Brian?

BRIAN : Well, what do you think?

3. POST MORTEM

(Scene: The Reception after the Funeral)

BRIAN : That was a 'lovely' funeral, if you can say that.

ALASTAIR : Lovely's not a word I'd use for a funeral, Brian.

BRIAN : Well, what would you call it?

(Silence)

BRIAN : How do you feel Margaret?

MARGARET : I felt all right until that sister of Jack's said
'Don't worry, you'll get over it!'

ALASTAIR : But that was a nice thing to say.

MARGARET : Alastair, I don't want to get **over** it .
My man's dead.
I am a widow.
My children don't have a father.
I'm not going to get **over** that.

ALASTAIR : Well, what are you going to do?
Dress in black and weep forever?

MARGARET : No. I'm going to go through it.
And I'm not going to go through it dressed in black.

BRIAN : Have you seen the doctor, Margaret?

MARGARET : What for? I'm perfectly healthy.

BRIAN : Well, sometimes a wee tranquiliser helps.
When our Mary lost her mother she was on valium for a
couple of months.

MARGARET : And what was she like when she came off valium?

BRIAN : Well, it was hard for her.

13

MARGARET :	Then I'd rather have it hard for me now . . . I don't intend to delay my grief for three months.	
ALASTAIR :	You're very brave, Margaret.	
MARGARET :	I don't like the word 'brave', Alastair. That's what folk say when you don't cry . . . especially when men don't cry. I don't think that's brave, I think that's being stubborn. Why choke up what should come out?	
BRIAN :	Well, whatever happens, you'll have your friends around you and Michael will not be long in taking his father's place . . . he's nearly fourteen now.	
MARGARET :	Brian, I hope to God that you never suggest to Michael that he should take Jack's place. He's a boy, not a man. He's my son, not my husband. I want him to stay my son, not try to be something he's not.	
BRIAN :	You're very hard, Margaret.	
MARGARET :	Sometimes you have to be: otherwise you become soft without being tender.	

4. THE CLOTHES

(Scene: Margaret's Home)

ALASTAIR :	I was just wondering, Margaret . . . if you need a hand with anything . . . don't be afraid to ask.
MARGARET :	Thank's Alastair, I probably will. I'll need a hand to get rid of Jack's clothes . . . maybe you'd like some . . . ?
ALASTAIR :	What? Me walk in my dead brother's shoes?
MARGARET :	And why not?
ALASTAIR :	Well, it just seems a bit odd. In any case, you'll be wanting to hang on to his things for a while.
MARGARET :	Why?

ALASTAIR : Just as a memento.

MARGARET : Alastair, Jack lives in my heart and in heaven.
He doesn't live in the socks, shoes and Y-fronts that are lying
in the bedroom cabinet.

ALASTAIR : No, I know that.

MARGARET : In any case, I've seen too many folk hanging on . . .
hanging on to the last paper he read,
the last cup he drank from,
never changing the bedroom where their man died . . .
I think that's morbid.

. . . Oh . . . and that's another thing, maybe you and Brian
would give me a hand with some decorating?

ALASTAIR : Decorating?

MARGARET : Yes . . . I'm going to paint the bedroom and the living room.

ALASTAIR : So soon after Jack's death? Margaret, what will your
relatives say?

MARGARET : Well it's quite obvious what you'll say.
You'll only feel happy if you see my face tripping me.
Just remember,
I had a good marriage and a good married life.
Jack didn't beat me or desert me or worry me,
he loved me.
If he never punished me when he was alive,
why should I want to look as if he's punishing me when he's
dead?

ALASTAIR : I don't quite understand.

MARGARET : No . . . you men are all the same.
You seem to think that, because a man dies, everybody who
depended upon him should stand still and mope forever.

ALASTAIR : Aye, well, I suppose life goes on.

MARGARET : Yes, Alastair, life goes on,
but only if you live it.

* * * * * * *

QUESTION TIME

Like I Beg Your Pardon, Question Time *requires people with some experience of acting and ability to immerse themselves in the characters, whether they be on stage or among the audience. It is also necessary that whoever plays Jesus looks nothing like the classical saviour, but more like a slightly bashful tradesman.*

The hall should be laid out, if possible, as for Question Time as presented on television. ROBIN NIGHT must speak as if to a camera, at least for the first three of four of his lines. When he gets flustered by the panellists he may want to make signs to the camera or stage crew that they should pull the plug out or somehow rescue him.

Characters:

ROBIN NIGHT	*... a polite but flusterable chairman.*
MARY BLACKHOUSE	*... a pious conservative purist.*
JOHNNY SNOT	*... an unmannerly punk.*
JESUS	
LADY CYNTHIA ST. JOHN STODDART-WEST	*... a semi-aristocrat.*
ALICE ANDERSON	*... a timid teenager.*
BILLY BOYNE	*... a rampant Orangeman from West of Scotland.*
HENRY GRAINGER	*... a sociology student.*

Scene: *The hall should be set as above. ROBIN, MARY and JOHNNY are in place behind a low table. Somewhere near by, but not evident, should be a spare chair JESUS can pick up in order to join the panel.*

MARY and JOHNNY sit to ROBIN'S left; JESUS to his right. The four other characters should be seated in the audience as unostentatiously as possible.

Props: *JESUS should carry an old bag in which are a saw, some letters, a mirror, a handkerchief and the pocket taken off an old pair of jeans. MARY should have a bible suitable for both quoting from and thumping JOHNNY, who can be covered in safety pins and have his hair coloured green or red.*

The end of the play is subdued and poignant. If the actors could manage it, it is good to finish with a song about Jesus sung by them all, but preferably in a calm mode and unaccompanied. Thuma Mina *from the* Freedom Is Coming *collection is very appropriate.*

* * * * * * *

VOICE OFF	:	All quiet please ! !
		Ten seconds . . . *(ROBIN adjusts his bow tie and MARY shuffles nervously while JOHNNY looks bored)*
		Five
		Four
		Three
		Two
		One
ROBIN	:	Good evening and welcome to Question Time which comes tonight from . . . . *(Name of venue)*
		My name is Robin Night, the panel's names you will learn in a minute and as for the people in the audience . . . your guess is as good as mine.
		On my left is Mrs. Mary Blackhouse, National Secretary of the Early To Bed And Don't Burp At The Table Society.
MARY	:	*(Fluttering)* Good evening.
ROBIN	:	On her left is Mr. Johnny Snott of the Poisoned Punks Against Everything Party.
JOHNNY	:	*(Burps, clears his throat or makes some unsavoury gesture)*
ROBIN	:	Well, now, let's get on with the . . .
		(At this point, JESUS walks gently on, passing across the platform, picking up the chair at the side and sitting on it. The others watch him with interest and surprise. ROBIN gapes.)
		. . . ahem . . . and on my right, a little late . . . but better late than never we have Mr. . . . ?
JESUS	:	*(Very softly)* Jesus.
ROBIN	:	*(Taken aback)* I'm sorry I didn't quite catch that. *(Moves closer to JESUS)* Could you say your name again?
JESUS	:	*(A little louder)* Jesus.
ROBIN	:	On my right we have *(Hesitatingly)* . . . Mr. . . . Jesus.
MARY	:	*(In an outburst)* But he's nothing like . . . ! *(Retracts and composes herself)* . . . I'm sorry.
ROBIN	:	Well, it looks as if we're going to have a lively evening. So, let's have the first question and it comes from Lady Cynthia St. John Stoddart-West, who is the Principal of the Churchill-Spencer Finishing School for Young Ladies.
		Are you in the audience Lady Cynthia?
		(She rises)
		Ah yes . . . there you are. Could we have your question please?

CYNTHIA	:	I would like to ask the panel who they think God would welcome first into heaven . . . Mrs. Margaret Thatcher or Neil Kinnock?
ROBIN	:	Lady Cynthia wants to know who God would welcome first into heaven, Mrs. Margaret Thatcher or Neil Kinnock.
		Do you have a particular reason for asking that question, Lady Cynthia?
CYNTHIA	:	Yes. Mrs. Thatcher is a friend of mine. Mr. Kinnock is not!
		(She sits)
ROBIN	:	Mary Blackhouse, can I put that question to you first of all. Who would God welcome first into heaven?
MARY	:	I appreciate Lady Cynthia's boldness in asking this very important question which I will answer with a text: *(Consults bible)* Romans 13, 2: 'Anyone who rebels against authority is resisting a divine institution; and those who resist have themselves to blame for the punishment they receive'.
		I have no doubt that St. Paul had Mr. Kinnock in mind when he wrote these words. No doubt whatsoever.
ROBIN	:	*(Interrupting)* But Mrs. Blackhouse, St. Paul died 1900 years before Mr. Kinnock was born.
MARY	:	That just goes to show that St. Paul was ahead of his time.
		I have no doubt in my mind that when the roll is called up yonder *(Looks upward)* Margaret Thatcher will be heaven's first foot.
ROBIN	:	*(Enthusiastically)* Well done, Mary . . . *(Retracts)* . . . I mean, thank you for being so frank Mrs. Blackhouse.
		Now Mr. Snot . . . or can I call you Johnny?
JOHNNY	:	Certainly 'Robin'.
ROBIN	:	Do you think God will welcome Mrs. Thatcher first?
JOHNNY	:	Well, much as I hate to agree with this old windbag sitting next to me, I think she's right.
ROBIN	:	Could you say why?
JOHNNY	:	Because I think God's right, don't I? I think God's a Tory.
		Stands to reason doesn't it? I mean to say, if God believed in real people . . . I mean real class people . . . like me . . . he wouldn't let this stupid government put 3 million people on the dole, would he? God must be a Tory.

ROBIN	:	I wonder if we could test audience reaction at this point. How many *(Stands up and goes to front)* . . . How many in the audience believe that God is a member of the Conservative Party?
		(Ad. Lib. some comment on the response)
		How many believe that God is a member of the Communist Party?
		(Ad. Lib. a comment . . .)
		It looks very much as if God is in the Scottish Nationalists.
		Well, let's move to the next question and it comes . . .
JOHNNY	:	*(Interrupting)* Here, shouldn't you ask him? *(Points to JESUS who looks quite calm and oblivious)* I mean, if he is who he says he is, he might have some inside information.
ROBIN	:	Well I . . . Well . . . eh . . . Well . . . Yes . . . of course . . . I was just going to . . .
		Ahem . . . Mr. . . . Jesus . . . would you like to say who will be welcomed first into heaven?
JESUS	:	*(Straight)* No.
ROBIN	:	*(A bit put out, chewing his tongue)*
		I'm sorry?
JESUS	:	No.
ROBIN	:	You wouldn't even like to make a guess?
JESUS	:	No.
ROBIN	:	Could you tell us why?
JESUS	:	*(Towards LADY CYNTHIA)* When there is so much on earth that you could do, why do you want to speculate on heaven which you have no control over?
ROBIN	:	*(Flustered)* . . . A good point . . . eh . . . point taken . . .
		Well *(To CYNTHIA)* does that answer your question Lady Cynthia St. John Stoddart-West?
CYNTHIA	:	*(Boldly)* No.
ROBIN	:	Good . . . then let's move on to the next question which comes from Miss Alice Anderson, a third year pupil at . . . . *(Name of a local school)*. And let's hope it's a little less controversial. Is Miss Anderson with us? *(She rises)* Can we have your question please?
ALICE	:	*(Shyly)* Is it all right to have sex before marriage?

19

ROBIN	:	*(Stunned)* . . . a bb . . . a . . . bb . . . Would you repeat the question?
ALICE	:	Is it all right . . . Is it all right to have sex before marriage?
ROBIN	:	The question is . . . **is it all right to have sex before marriage?**
JOHNNY	:	*(Butts in before he is asked)* . . . Of course it is . . . as long as you take precautions . . . pull the curtains, lock the door . . . know what I mean?
MARY	:	*(Assaulting JOHNNY with her handbag while ROBIN panics)* Young man! . . . this is outrageous . . . outrageous and depraved . . . Have you never heard 1st Corinthians 6, 19? *(Consulting bible)* 'The fornicator sins against his own body'.
JOHNNY	:	Hey, leave it out, leave it out, I was only joking!
MARY	:	Indeed I have left it out. There's far too much of it going on these days. Spare the rod and spoil the child . . . that's what I say. Why when I was a girl, my father used to beat me . . . beat me . . . beat me if I so much as **looked** at a man.
JOHNNY	:	Does that mean you met your husband on a blind date?
MARY	:	*(Assaulting him again)* . . . Impudence . . . sheer impudence and anarchy and lasciviousness and licenteousness and lustfulness. Fornication . . . that's the only thing you have in your mind.
ROBIN	:	*(Gets up to pull MARY off)* Thank you . . . eh . . . thank you Mrs. Blackhouse. Now can we have the next question . . . ?
JOHNNY	:	Hoi . . . what about him? Aren't you going to ask him?
ROBIN	:	Who?
JOHNNY	:	Jesus.
ROBIN	:	*(Embarassed)* I don't think we really need to . . . I mean, sex isn't the kind of thing you would talk to Jesus about is it?
JESUS	:	Why not? I'm completely human. I know about sex as I know about faith and love.
ROBIN	:	Yes . . . of course . . . Well, Jesus . . . Would you like to tell Miss Anderson if she should have sex before marriage?

JESUS	:	No.
ROBIN	:	I'm sorry?
JESUS	:	No . . . I won't tell her.

But I'd like to ask her why she wants someone else to make a decision that she should be responsible for?

And I'd want to ask her if she knows anything about love?

ROBIN : Well, it's getting hot in here . . . *(Rubbing neck)* . . . I wonder if we could move quickly to the next question which comes from Billy Boyne who is a member of the . . . . *(Local Name)* branch of Rangers Supporter's Club.

Could you make it brief please, Mr. Boyne?

BILLY : *(Standing up)*
Right . . . here it is . . . short and snappy . . . four words . . .
Is God a Catholic?

ROBIN : I'm sorry, I don't understand.

BILLY : I just want it settled once and for all.
I know we're right because I know King Billy was right. And it's time that everybody got it right.
So I want it answered once and for all . . .
Is God a Catholic?

ROBIN : *(Trembling)* . . . Mmmmary . . . Mary Blackhouse.

MARY : *(Confidently)*
I feel sure . . . that God is . . . an Anglican.

For when I read Psalm 121, 'I will lift up mine eyes unto the hills' . . . I immediately think of the Yorkshire Dales. I'm sure that's where the author was thinking of when he wrote these beautiful words.
I can picture the steep slopes with that lovely little Edwardian church perched on a grassy knoll . . . and when I look at it, a tear comes to my eye and deep inside . . . deep inside . . . I know . . . that God . . . is . . . an Anglican.

ROBIN : Mrs. Blackhouse, I'm not sure how to tell you . . .
but David . . . the man who wrote some of the Psalms, didn't live in Yorkshire. He never saw the Dales.

MARY : *(Indignantly)* Didn't he?

ROBIN : No . . . in fact, he didn't speak English.

MARY : Good heavens. How uncivilised of him!

ROBIN : Well Johnny, . . . do you have any opinion as to whether or not God is a Catholic?

21

JOHNNY	:	I don't actually . . . that's what puts me off God . . . you know what I mean . . . all that fighting between Catholics and Protestants. I think it's a lot of nonsense. Know what I mean?

I'm an ecumenical atheist, actually.
What I think is that *(Here he speaks warmly in order to surprise at the end)* . . . all the Catholics and all the Anglicans,
and all the Baptists and all the Presbyterians,
and all the Episcopalians and all the Congregationalists
should get together.
They should unite . . .
they should join together . . .
and fight the Salvation Army ! ! ! ! !

(MARY assaults him with her bag and appropriate noises)

ROBIN : Ahem . . . thank you Johnny.

Now, I won't forget **you** this time, Jesus.

Would you like to answer Billy Boyne's question?

JESUS : No.

ROBIN : I thought you might say that.

JESUS : *(Standing up)* . . . But I would like to ask Billy Boyne when he's going to stop hiding behind his orange sash and start loving his neighbour?
(Holds a silence with his eyes, then sits.)

ROBIN : . . . eh . . . has that answered your question, Mr. Boyne?

BILLY : Certainly not . . . and who does he think he is talking about my orange sash . . . just who does . . .

ROBIN : *(Interrupting)* Well, well . . . I see we have a little disagreement on that issue. Let's hope our last question will have a more unanimous response.
It comes from Mr. Henry Grainger who is a student reading sociology at the University of . . . . *(Name)*

HENRY : I want to ask whether, in view of the horrendous nature of the medical, nutritional and socio-economic disorders in the Sahel and Eritrean regions, it is possible to postulate with any credibility that some omniscient and omnipotent deity is the beneficient Ground of all being?

ROBIN : *(Gasps)* Yes . . . well I wonder who can help us out?

Indeed I wonder who understands the question?

JESUS : Excuse me.
I think he was asking how there could be a God of love when people are dying of hunger in Ethiopia.

ROBIN	:	Exactly . . . I was just about to say that.
		Mrs. Blackhouse . . . can there be a God of love when people are dying in Ethiopia?
MARY	:	Well . . . of course there is. It's just that it's their own fault. I mean . . . they're underdeveloped. If they had stayed part of the British Empire, all would have been well. But now they don't have a government like ours which ensures that all are fed and watered.
		(JOHNNY makes a raspberry)
		Oh you may make rude noises . . . but it's quite true. As it says in Exodus 20, 5: 'I punish the children for the sins of the fathers to the third and fourth generation of those who hate me.'
ROBIN	:	Eh . . . Mrs. Blackhouse. . . I hate to say it but . . .
		Well, first of all, Ethiopia was never in the British Empire, so it never left it. And, secondly, in Exodus, Moses was talking to the Jews about idolatry, not to the Africans about famine.
MARY	:	That makes no difference to me and I'm sure it wouldn't to Moses.
ROBIN	:	What about you, Johnny? Do you think there can be a God of love when people are starving in Ethiopia?
JOHNNY	:	*(As JOHNNY speaks, JESUS takes out a handkerchief and wipes his eyes, gently)*
		No . . . that and the protestant—catholic bit . . . that's what puts me off religion. How can he be a God of love? . . . I mean to say . . . where is he? . . . Where is he when people are dying of hunger?
ROBIN	:	Perhaps we should put that to you, Jesus. Where is God in a world where people are dying of malnutrition?
JESUS	:	I have just come from Ethiopia . . . that's why I was late. I came also from Nicaragua and South Africa and I've been in Northern Ireland.
		I have just come from the places where God is . . . Waiting . . . Waiting for those who call themselves Christians to go and meet him.

ROBIN	:	*(After a pause)* Well, time's run out . . . but I wonder, since you *(JESUS)* are here . . . I wonder if I could ask you a question? The 'eternal life' bit . . . how do you . . . get it? I mean . . . how do I get it . . . eternal life . . . ?
JESUS	:	Do you believe?
ROBIN	:	Oh yes . . . I believe . . . I was converted at 2.30 on 29th Sept. 1964. I became a Sunday School Teacher and then an Elder. I have a wife, two children, a luxury bungalow and a catamaran on the Clyde. I'm a Free Mason, a member of the Rotary Club . . . .
JESUS	:	*(Interrupting)* And are you happy? Deep down, are you really happy?
ROBIN	:	*(Sadly)* No. How do I get the kind of life you talk about?
JESUS	:	I will not answer your question. Instead I will give you a present. Indeed I will give a present to all those who asked questions. *(Gives ROBIN a pocket)* To you I'll give one of my pockets . . . . .
ROBIN	:	*(Looks)* . . . But it's got a hole in it!
JESUS	:	Yes . . . that's right. All my pockets have holes in them. You have so much . . . this will help you to have less and, at the end of the day, to have more. Cynthia *(She comes down to the front)* To you I give my carpenter's saw. For you, like many others, like to speculate about heaven, but do nothing to change things on earth. *(Gives saw)* Alice *(She comes forward)* Alice, I want to give you some letters to read . . . Letters that disillusioned teenagers sent me who discovered too late that it is a mistake to give your body before you are able to give your heart. *(Gives letters)* Billy *(He comes)* Billy, here is a mirror. You have to learn to love your neighbour as yourself. That means that you have first to learn to love yourself . . . and not hide behind a badge or scarf or sash. *(Gives the mirror)*

And Henry *(He comes)*

Henry . . . to you I give my handkerchief.
It is wet with my tears and with God's tears, and with the
tears of the poor and the hungry among whom God sits and
waits. *(Gives handkerchief)*

And, Henry, it will never get dry until you and others like you
move to meet God in the places where you imagine he is
absent.

*(All leave during quiet music
or they may sing)*

* * * * * * *

I BEG YOUR PARDON

This is a short play about forgiveness. It may be used as a prelude to a discussion on that issue, or as a presentation in church as an alternative to a sermon.

For best effect, the four main characters should be seated near to and in the middle of the four walls of the hall or church, so that they speak across the audience to each other. They should also sit either facing the wall or perpendicular to it and, when they speak, turn or rise to face the audience.

In the centre of the hall, or at a designated spot, should be three vacant chairs, next to each other and facing MAGNUS'S chair. The other three main characters occupy them towards the end of the play.

JESUS should be sitting incognito among the audience with a bunch of flowers concealed from view.

MARTIN, MAWDY, MIRANDA and MAGNUS should be dressed as suits their social situation. JESUS should not appear as particularly messianic.

Throughout the play it is advisable to have a line of music, which may be either vocal or instrumental, repeated as indicated in order to break up the dialogue. If the play is not going to lead to discussion immediately, meditative music or a song is best to follow rather than applause.

***Note:** This play, more than the others in this collection, requires people who are skilled or experienced in acting to convey its meaning. MAGNUS particularly needs to be in command of his long speech and tell it as a story rather than as memorised lines.*

* * * * * * *

(A tune is heard which can bear repeating or improvisation, during which the four main characters appear from a doorway. MARTIN enters, followed by MIRANDA, MAWDY and MAGNUS, walking as befits their station. Once in position, they stand facing the audience. Their intial speech is factual and dispassionate.)

MARTIN	:	Martin.
MIRANDA	:	Miranda.
MAWDY	:	Mawdy.
MAGNUS	:	Magnus.
MARTIN	:	Age 19.
MIRANDA	:	Age 24.
MAWDY	:	Age 31.
MAGNUS	:	Age 58.

MARTIN	:	Taught.
MIRANDA	:	Touched.
MAWDY	:	Transformed.
MAGNUS	:	Told.

(Music . . . . They all sit)

MARTIN : Martin, age 19,
van boy, croupier, assistant animal breeder . . .
Not now though . . .
Taught.

MIRANDA : Miranda, age 24,
weaver, would-be mother, hostess . . .
But not any more . . .
Touched.

MAWDY : Mawdy, age 31,
street trader
. . . once upon a time,
. . . once upon a long time – though a short time ago.
But no longer.
Transformed.

MAGNUS : Magnus. age 58,
farmer, business man, councillor, father.
Told.

(Music – a few bars)

MARTIN : Martin . . . that was my grandfather's name and it was my
father's idea to call me that.
Most things to do with me and my future were my father's
ideas.
I was conditioned, pre-packed, pigeon-holed.
It was to be like father, like son . . .
but not this son, not this Martin.

MIRANDA : I was christened Sharon.
I suppose it's a nice name, but it's a bit old fashioned. So I
changed it to Miranda.
I thought it sounded better.

MAGNUS : *(Interrupting in disgust while seated, but with head turning round)*
Tell them the truth ! !

MIRANDA : *(Defensively and obviously ruffled)*
. . . I thought Miranda sounded better.

MAWDY : I don't know why I'm called Mawdy.
It's a silly kind of name, especially when they call me 'poor
Mawdy' or 'poor wee Mawdy'.

MAGNUS : *(Interrupting as before)*   or 'Mawdy the Minker' ! !

27

MAWDY	:	*(Unruffled)* . . . or 'Mawdy the Minker' . . . or even **'Old Mawdy'**.

Imagine calling me . . . old . . . me at 31?
They think they know me, but it's me who knows them.
They've only seen me, but I've watched them . . . sat and
watched them and know more than they think I can imagine
. . . them that call me 'Poor Mawdy' or 'Old Mawdy' . . . yes
and even 'Mawdy the Minker'.

MAGNUS	:	I'm called Magnus after my grandfather and I'm proud of it. He started the business and built the farm. And I stand in his shoes in the hope that one day someone will stand in mine.

(Music – a few bars)

MARTIN	:	I called myself a van boy . . . well that was right . . . for six weeks . . . and I have been helping out with animal breeding . . . for about 10 days now.

I said I was a croupier. That means somebody who spins the
wheel and deals the cards in a casino.
I was only the croupier when the man who did it went for a
leak. The rest of the time I bought the chips and played the
cards . . . and lost the money.

Of course it would have been different if I had done what my
father told me . . . if I had been a good boy.

But I wasn't a 'good boy'.
I wasn't even 'one of the lads'.
I was a bad boy.

MIRANDA	:	I said I was a weaver . . . well I was a weaver. And I still am a would-be mother, but it'll only ever be 'would-be'. . . because I found out that I can't be. I'm sterile . . . infertile . . . and I'm not sure that I like men anyway.

(As she stops speaking, MAWDY looks at her and speaks gently)

MAWDY	:	You can tell them, Mandy.
MAGNUS	:	Mandy? Randy ! ! ! Tell them the truth . . . Randy!
MIRANDA	:	As I said, I don't really like men, even though I'm now a hostess.
MAGNUS	:	*(Scoffing)* A hostess? A whore ! ! ! *(He gets to his feet)* Tell them you're a whore And a cheap one at that Randy ! !

(She sits . . . silence)

(Realising he is still on his feet and has an audience)

28

```
                    I am a farmer and a business man
                    And a councillor and a father
                    And that's all.
MAWDY     :    I think I should say that I'm not really a street trader. I'm a
               beggar ... or used to be.
               There wasn't much else I could do. You see, I couldn't walk.
               So I just sat still and sometimes would sell things ... clothes-
               pegs or matches or pencils. But I discovered that I got more by
               not having anything to sell.
               Folk put more in my cap when they saw that I couldn't do
               anything in return.
               Funny that ... isn't it?
```

(Music — a few bars)

MARTIN   :   Martin, 19. I work with animals.
               Taught.

MIRANDA   :   Mandy, 24, hostess.
               Touched.

MAWDY   :   Mawdy, 31, beggar.
               Transformed.

MAGNUS   :   Magnus, 58,
               farmer, businessman, councillor, father.
               Told.

(Music — a few bars)

MAWDY   :   I suppose I should say something about the transformation.

MAGNUS   :   *(Interrupting)* I wouldn't bother. Don't bore people!

MAWDY   :   *(Unruffled)*
               It began in my legs ..... they move now ... as you see.
               (moves his legs)
               I never thought that would happen.
               Never in the 25 years I sat with my cap at the side of the
               street, did I think I'd walk.
               I used to imagine what it would feel like and I decided one day
               that it was maybe better not to be able to move.
               You see, there's a funny comfort in being a beggar.
               It's the comfort of having no responsibility, because you've
               got no status.
               But now they move ... and I can move ... that's the
               transformation ... in them ... in me ... you understand?

MIRANDA   :   *(Taking up from Mawdy enthusiastically)*
               It's true ...
               I've seen the difference.
               I've known Mawdy for years.

He used to sit opposite where I stood.
Then one day he stood opposite where I sat . . . .
It was terrible.

I was a crumpled, wasted heap.

MAGNUS : *(Interrupting)*
You were a filthy bitch ! !

MIRANDA : I was too terrified to cry.
I had my hands over my ears.
I didn't want to hear all these polite men who called me a
woman of pleasure, making sure they got the last laugh.

MAGNUS : *(More angrily)*
You were a filthy bitch ! !

MIRANDA : They cursed me. They kicked me.
They had their dogs ready to set on me.
And then somebody touched me.
And he told those who had got on where to get off.

It's true, Mawdy, isn't it?

MAWDY : Aye, it's true, Mandy.

(Music — a few bars)

MIRANDA : Mandy, age 24.
Touched.

MAWDY : Mawdy, age 31.
Transformed.

(pause)

MARTIN : Martin, age 19 . . . . Taught.

"Taught by experience?" you ask . . .

Oh yes, experience is a great teacher . . .

Three months in jail for embezzling money;
£4000 to pay off in gambling debts;
two women in the family way —
and a dose of gonorrhoea . . .
. . . experience is a great teacher.
But not the greatest.

It was a story.

It was the day I'd gone to the circus to see if I could make
money on anything . . . darts . . . guns . . . anything.
And I got nowhere, but ended up in a tent where somebody
was telling stories.

I listened. It was strange.

30

I could have written the story . . .
because it was about . . . it was . . . me.

. . . leave home, . . . run away to the bright lights
. . . try to make a fortune . . . end up a complete loser.

That was the story . . .
. . . apart from the last bit.
The last bit told me what to do,
but I don't know if I can.

The last bit is about going back . . . home.

But if I leave my cheap wine and cheap women,
if I leave the pig sty and hoof it home,
will my father fling open the front door and run out
. . . and throw his arms round me and say "Come in, come in"?

Will my father do that?   *(He sits. A pause)*

MAGNUS   :   *(Sitting as he speaks, and speaking in the direction of his chair)*

Magnus, age 58,
farmer, businessman, councillor, father.
Told.

(Music – during this music the other three leave their places and come together in the middle, where they stand at the prescribed location)

MARTIN   :   Martin, 19, taught.

MIRANDA   :   Mandy, 24, touched.

MAWDY   :   Mawdy, 31, transformed.

         (They look to Magnus who sits motionless)

MARTIN   :   Father ? ? ? ! ! !

*(They sit . . . a pause . . . MAGNUS stands and speaks.
At first he is matter of fact, but gradually he becomes more humane,
even sentimental, until the end of his speech.)*

MAGNUS   :   This morning, I was on my way to do the 'Sunday Thing'.

'The Sunday Thing' . . . that's all I ever called it . . . ever since
I was a child and my grandfather would come into the kitchen
at quarter past ten and say 'Time for the Sunday Thing'.

So we would file out of the house . . . me first, being the
youngest, then my two sisters, then my three older brothers,
then my mother and father and finally my grandfather,
holding a bunch of flowers.

We would walk single-file down to the edge of the field, along
the burn *(stream)*, and up to the white bridge. There we would
ford the burn by skipping over the stones, while the grown-
ups crossed by the bridge.

Then we'd get back into line and walk single-file to the church gate.
I'd stop first, then the others;
and my grandfather would come last.
He would walk past us and cross first over the gravel to the church door, with us all following in reverse order.

It would be half-past ten.
Nobody was ever about except the organist if his bus was early.

My grandfather would lead the procession right down to the front and we'd all line up before the Communion table *(Altar)*.
Then he would walk forward to put the flowers in the vase in the middle of the table in memory of his mother and father and his wife, my grandmother, and two of their children who had died in infancy.

We'd stand for a moment in silence and then shuffle into the family pew.

That was the 'Sunday Thing' . . .
and we always did it the same way . . . and nobody bothered . . . well, they wouldn't, would they, seeing as we were the wealthiest family in the church and had helped to build and rebuild the place.

When my grandfather died, the custom continued.
I'd still be first out the house with my older brothers and sisters behind me and my mother and father last.

My father would put the flowers in the vase in memory of his parents and his sisters who died when they were children . . . and then also in memory of my mother . . . and then also in memory of my two brothers who were killed during the war.

And when my father died, I took over.
I would say at 10.15, "Time for the Sunday Thing" . . .
and we'd go out . . .
my two sons first, then my wife
and me carrying the flowers.

And that happened every week until, one by one,
they dropped off . . . or ran off . . .
my wife with another man . . .
my younger son . . . *(Points)* . . . you, Martin, with half my money . . .
my older son . . . he just stopped going.
So I did it myself . . . like this morning.

I left the house, walked down the field,
along the burn, over the bridge,
across the gravel, into the church . . .

and I was just about to put the flowers into the vase,
when a hand pulled at my arm and a voice said . . .

JESUS : *(Quickly interrupting. As he speaks he moves forward to behind the three others. He carries a bunch of flowers in his hand.)*

No, Magnus!

Don't put an offering on the altar before God
if in your heart you hold something
against your neighbour,
      your son,
         or the woman you called a filthy bitch,
         especially when you helped to foul her.

First go and make it up to your neighbour,
         to your son,
           and to the woman you called a whore
           and used as a whore.

Then, having forgiven them,
and having been forgiven by them,
go and offer your gift,
and God will forgive you.

*(MAGNUS, who has been looking at JESUS, sits down
and looks straight ahead, obviously annoyed.)*

MAWDY : *(Speaking to MAGNUS, as do the others)*

Forgive . . .
That's what he did
and he transformed my legs . . . and my life.

MIRANDA : Forgive . . .
That's what he did when he touched me.

MARTIN : Forgive . . .
That's what he taught me to do
and to expect.

(Pause . . . . Then MAGNUS stands and looks at JESUS.)

MAGNUS : Give me back my flowers!

JESUS : Give them back their dignity.

(MAGNUS stares, then sits, turning away from them.

*They get up, one by one and go over to touch him on the shoulder,
MARTIN first, then MIRANDA, then MAWDY, then JESUS.
They file out slowly in the same order.*

*MAGNUS gets up and makes to leave in the opposite direction.
Suddenly he turns and runs after the other four.)*

* * * * * * *

33

GOD AND MAN AND WOMAN

This can be read by two people standing apart,
allowing for pauses for thought and laughter as appropriate.

A   :   In the beginning, God made man.
He was so disappointed that he tried again,

and the next time, he made woman.

B   :   Eve, the first woman, was a vegetarian.
She liked apples, and ate the wrong one.

Men have been suspicious of vegetarians ever since.

A   :   Noah didn't eat apples.
He was a man . . . so he drank alchohol.
In fact, he drank so much alchohol that one day
        his sons found their old man completely sozzled
        and lying in the nude.

Women have been suspicious of alchohol ever since.

B   :   Lot didn't eat apples or drink wine.
He just lived in a city where the men didn't know who they
fancied. So God told him to leave the city, and so he did.
God said, 'Don't look back, for I'm going to burn down the city.'
So Lot didn't look back, but his wife did
and she turned into a pillar of salt.

Women have never looked back since.

A   :   Delilah didn't eat apples, drink wine or look back.
She was a hairdresser.
Samson didn't know that,
        but while he was resting his macho muscles,
        Delilah cut his hair and took his strength away.

Men have avoided being bald ever since.

B   St. Paul didn't know Eve, Noah, Lot or Delilah.
But he did know some women,
     and those he did must have given him bad memories.
Because he told them not to speak in church,
     not to go into a church without a hat
     and always to obey their husbands.
Paul also said that men shouldn't get married
     unless they were unable to control themselves.

Men have been unable to control themselves ever since.

A   :   But Jesus was different.

He was strong, but he cried.
He even cried in front of other men.
He knew that some women had bad reputations,
     but that didn't keep him back from them:
     he knelt beside them.

He loved his disciples who were all men
     and he wasn't afraid to tell them that he loved them.
And though he was never married,
     he was always surrounded by women who, at his death,
     were more faithful to him than the men.

Jesus didn't make a fuss about who was who, or who was what.
He said that everyone who loved him was his mother,
                        his sister,
                        his brother.

A & B :   Thank God for Jesus.

* * * * * *

CURRENT PUBLICATIONS OF THE IONA COMMUNITY

PEACE AND ADVENTURE   ISBN 0 9501351 6 X
Ellen Murray

THROUGH WOOD AND NAILS   Record No.146/REC/S
THROUGH WOOD AND NAILS   Cassette No.IC/WGP/001
Iona Abbey

THE WHOLE EARTH SHALL CRY GLORY   Paperback ISBN 0 947988 00 9
THE WHOLE EARTH SHALL CRY GLORY   Hardback ISBN 0 947988 04 1
Iona prayers by Rev. George F. MacLeod

WILD GOOSE PRINTS No.1   ISBN 0 947988 06 8
John Bell & Graham Maule

WHAT IS THE IONA COMMUNITY?   ISBN 0 947988 07 6
Iona Community

A TOUCHING PLACE   Cassette No.IC/WGP/004
Wild Goose Worship Group

A TOUCHING PLACE   ISBN 0 947988 09 2
John Bell & Graham Maule

WILD GOOSE PRINTS No.2   ISBN 0 947988 10 6
John Bell & Graham Maule

COLUMBA – The Man & The Myth   ISBN 0 947988 11 4
Mitchell Bunting

IN PRAISE OF GOD'S GOODNESS   ISBN 0 947988 12 2
Kathryn Galloway

FOLLY AND LOVE   Cassette No.IC/WGP/005
FOLLY AND LOVE   ISBN 0 947988 15 7
Iona Abbey

90 RECIPES FROM THE IONA COMMUNITY   ISBN 0 947988 17 3
Sue Pattison

GRACE AND DYSENTERY   ISBN 0 947988 19 X
Ron Ferguson

EH ... JESUS ... YES, PETER ...?   ISBN 0 947988 20 3
John Bell & Graham Maule

FREEDOM IS COMING   Cassette No.IC/WGP/006
FREEDOM IS COMING   ISBN 91 86788 15 7
Utryck

CLOTH FOR THE CRADLE   Cassette No.IC/WGP/007
Wild Goose Worship Group

AT GROUND LEVEL   ISBN 0 947988 21 1
Ruth Burgess & Sally Carlaw

CO-OPERATION VERSUS EXPLOITATION   ISBN 0 947988 22 X
Walter Fyfe

WILD GOOSE SONGS – VOLUME 1   ISBN 0 947988 23 8
John Bell & Graham Maule

WILD GOOSE PRINTS No.3   ISBN 0 947988 24 6
John Bell & Graham Maule

THE CORACLE – REBUILDING THE COMMON LIFE   ISBN 0 947988 25 4
Jubilee reprint of Foundation Documents of the Iona Community

GOVAN OLD PARISH CHURCH   ISBN 0 947988 26 2
John Harvey

WILD GOOSE SONGS – VOLUME 2   ISBN 0 947988 27 0
John Bell & Graham Maule

THE IONA COMMUNITY WORSHIP BOOK   ISBN 0 947988 28 9
Iona Community

RE-INVENTING THEOLOGY   ISBN 0 947988 29 7
Ian M. Fraser

MEANING THE LORD'S PRAYER   ISBN 0 947988 30 0
George T. H. Reid